FOR A SPLENDID SUNNY APOCALYPSE

FOR A SPLENDID SUNNY APOCALYPSE
为一个阳光灿烂的世界末日而作

Selected Poetry of

Jiang Tao
姜涛

Translated from Chinese by **Josh Stenberg**

Zephyr Press | Brookline, Mass.

Cover image by Chung H. Chak
[tanuskithacat@gmail.com]
Book design by typeslowly
Printed by Bookmobile

The Translator's Foreword is based on the entry on Jiang Tao
written by the translator for *Dictionary of Literary Biography: Volume 387*
(Chinese Poets since 1949), edited by Christopher Lupke and Thomas E. Moran.

The poems "opera info," "winter solstice," "to the ends of the earth,"
and "things that travel by night" appeared in the *Harvard Review.*

Zephyr Press acknowledges with gratitude the financial support of
the Massachusetts Cultural Council and The Academy of American
Poets with funds from the Amazon Literary Partnership Poetry Fund.

Zephyr Press, a non-profit arts and education 501(c)(3) organization, publishes literary
titles that foster a deeper understanding of cultures and languages. Zephyr Press books
are distributed to the trade by Consortium Book Sales and Distribution [www.cbsd.com].

Cataloguing-in publication data is available from the Library of Congress.

ZEPHYR PRESS
www.zephyrpress.org

CONTENTS

Translator's Foreword

Jiang Tao 姜涛 is an author of poetry and literary criticism as well as a professor at Peking University, where he teaches modern poetry and culture. His work expresses profound malaise about the state of China, the world, and at times the human condition. The vehicle for these bleak observations is poetry notable for its good-humored self-deprecation and self-mockery.

The poet's restraint and subtlety, along with the moderate pace and size of his output, may justify the critic Zhang Jieyu's 张洁宇 admiring characterization of Jiang Tao as a "jogger," a poet who is "neither prolific, nor pitched to a lofty key" and who "frequently makes use of his particular style of self-mockery to conceal the seriousness, passion and melancholy that accompanies the way he deals with poetry."

Though Jiang Tao's work resists facile categorization, he has sometimes been considered an "intellectual poet" or a member of the Academic Group Xueyuan pai 学院派 based on his university career. Such categorizations place him alongside contemporaries such as Zhou Zan 周瓒, Zang Di 臧棣, and Leng Shuang 冷霜, all of whom he has known for decades. The contested term "academic" rightly suggests the erudition and wide range of reference deployed in Jiang Tao's work, his poetry also, in the words of critic Yang Xiaobin 杨小滨, "demonstrates the subtle satire the superficially 'academic' style can achieve," with campus locations and situations providing a springboard for incisive and sometimes caustic commentary on modern daily life.

Born on 21 December 1970 in Tianjin to parents who were both engineers, Jiang Tao was raised by a paternal uncle's family until the age of four. An only child, he was given to imagining and acting out heroic stories in solitude and began self-directed reading in modern Chinese and Western poetry and fiction beginning in middle school. Jiang Tao's interest in poetry was spurred at age sixteen by a chance encounter with *A Selection of Misty Poetry* 朦胧诗选, at which point he began to read publications such as *International Poetry Forum* 国际诗坛 and *A Selection of*

Symbolist Poetry 象征派诗选. Alongside what he considers "innumerable" Chinese influences, including recent, Republican-era, and classical figures, the most prominent foreign influences on his verse are T. S. Eliot and W. H. Auden.

Enrolling at Tsinghua University in 1989, Jiang Tao declared an undergraduate major in biomedical engineering. He found the university atmosphere dreary until he became involved with the Tsinghua Literary Society. Under the influence of classmates, Jiang Tao began to write poetry in his undergraduate years. Starting in 1991 he worked as chief editor on two issues of the unauthorized Tsinghua campus journal *Poetry Bulletin* 诗歌通讯. As president of the society from 1991 to 1994, he also took on the editorship of the campus poetry journal *Same Direction* 同方 from 1993 to 1994.

Jiang Tao abandoned engineering after his first degree and instead began his formal involvement in Chinese literary studies, writing a master's thesis in the Chinese department of Tsinghua University on the 1940s Photographicist 摄影主义 poets before leaving academia for two years to work as an editor at *China Culture Daily* 中国文化报, an organ of the Ministry of Culture. This job provided Jiang Tao with the income and time necessary for a period of sustained poetic work. In 1999, he embarked on doctoral studies at Peking University. Obtaining his Ph.D. in 2003 with a dissertation on Republican-era poetry, he remained in the department as an instructor. He has continued his association with the institution, becoming a member of the Modern Literature Research Group; he reached the rank of professor in 2020.

In 1997 Jiang Tao was awarded the Liu Li'an Poetry Prize, the earliest and leading prize for avant-garde verse. As a graduate student, he published works in prominent underground journals. Although his first collection of poetry was not placed with a publisher until 2005, his work became well-known in poetry circles because of his literary activities and two collections that he self-published with friends, *Sometimes to Mourn* (哀恸有时, 1994) and *Selections by Four Poets* (四人诗选, 1997). At about the same time that his poetry was being recognized in Beijing literary circles, his 1998 essay "Contemporary Poetry in Narrative" 叙述中

的当代诗歌 initiated his prolific and highly regarded critical contribution to work on contemporary Chinese poetry.

Formally, Jiang Tao's poetry has evolved over time. The bulk of his production shows a preference for lines, stanzas, and poems of short to middling length, while his early verse was largely arranged in longer poem suites. Since 1998, his poetry has grown more restrained in length and density of image, with the notable exception of the ten-part suite "Our Beautiful Life Together" 我们共同的美好生活, written in 2008, in which he explores his core themes of memory, the passing of time, and the relationship of poetry to reality. Stylistically, Jiang Tao often opts for the structurally and sometimes grammatically ambiguous, using subtle and unsettling shifts of tone and perspective. Seldom directly political or fulsomely lyrical, Jiang Tao instead is notable for extended complex metaphors, juxtapositions, and wry, dispassionate observation.

Consider the sleepers of "One Night at College", with its packed suggestions of adolescent eros, cosmopolitan intellectual ferment, wilful ignorance, mephitic thought:

> they are sleeping under blades of grass, sleeping by the telephone
> sleeping on the lake's still surface and high in the water tower
> they even sleep in garbage bags
> dilated pores exuding
> crude foreign lingo and sinful floral scents

> 他们睡在草叶下，睡在电话边
> 睡在静静的湖面和高高的水塔上
> 他们甚至睡在了垃圾袋里
> 张大的毛孔，渗出过
> 粗鲁的外语和罪孽的花香

His voice tends to be that of a measured, and solitary bystander, with a pronounced preference for sardonicism over transcendence. Speech or dialogue seldom appear and the tendency to colloquial language prominent in much contemporary mainland Chinese poetry is not pronounced. Unsurprisingly for a writer who went directly from his studies to teaching, the environment and dynamics of the campus sometimes come to the fore in locales and images. This tendency is evident in the opening of "Peach Blossoms Outside the Library" 图书馆前的桃花, written in 1995 while Jiang Tao was still a master's student:

> peach blossoms outside the library are bound to rebloom
> suffer all the insect damage and plaudits
> like tiny overdue books, one after the other
> thumbed to the final page by bicycle bells

> 图书馆前的桃花注定又要开放
> 历尽虫蛀和赞美
> 仿佛一本本过期的小书
> 被自行车的铃声，翻到了最后一页

Another example is found in the beginning of "One Night at College" 高校一夜), written in 2005

> but what has changed, green mountains
> still soar over the sports track
> campus is still bisected, yin and yang
> everyone's fast asleep anyhow

> 究竟什么发生了改变，青山
> 依旧飞过了操场
> 校园还是划分了阴阳
> 所有人，还是那样在沉睡

in which the lofty optimism of education seems to have been replaced or derided by a campus full of sleeping figures.

A resident of Beijing since his teenage years, Jiang Tao is also a peripatetic writer, traveling frequently within and outside of mainland China, often with other poet friends. Visits to Xinjiang, Qinghai, Mongolia, Turkey, Berlin, and Switzerland, often for literary festivals, have marked his poetry. In 2009 he was named to a two-year position at Nihon University in Tokyo, teaching in the College of Arts and Sciences and giving guest lectures at various Japanese universities and literary societies. In 2017 I had the good fortune to work with Jiang Tao through a Luce Foundation Chinese Poetry & Translation Fellowship at the Vermont Studio Center.

For more than a decade, Jiang Tao has also enjoyed a productive relationship with Taiwanese poetry and university circles. Jiang Tao first visited Taiwan in 2007, for Academia Sinica's Cross-Strait Post-Modern Poetics Conference, before becoming a visiting associate professor at Taiwan's National Tsing Hua University from 2015–2016. There, he taught in the Chinese department and participated in the Taipei Poetry Festival, the Pacific Poetry Festival, and events at the Qi Dong Poetry Salon both as a poet and literary historian and critic.

This cosmopolitanism and travel experience generates the tragicomedy of Chinese tourism in "Noseki Beach," where "the incoming tide carries off a nikon camera" or among the misbehaving confreres in the Taiwanese Hengchun peninsula, where the "polite seawater" delivers one of them "back to shore, time and again."

Jiang Tao's willingness to discomfit the reader is apparent in the way that his writing engages with various aspects of contemporary China. Themes that emerge include rural-urban migration; Chinese suburban lifestyle; and increasing materialism, wastefulness, and hypocrisy. Given that his vision of urban life is to a considerable extent one of isolation and miscommunication, it is no surprise that the rapid technological development of recent years receives skeptical treatment. Doubt about the gains in affluence of the Reform Era seem to be expressed in poems such as "A Day in the Cave" 洞中一日, written in 2011 and revised in 2015:

> living high enough now
> if you stretched out your hand seems like you could touch
> snow on the cave roof (this new apartment
> is a lot like a cave no matter how you look at it)

> 现如今，住的是足够高了
> 仿佛伸一伸手，就能摸到
> 洞顶的雪（这新房
> 怎么看都更像一个山洞）

Here the convenient modern apartment—the aspiration of the young city-dweller—is reduced to troglodytism. Some early poems contain an echo of the dynamism of the 1990s, while later poems cast a disdainful eye on a youthful past. Individual poems shift craftily between wistfulness and satire. This passage is from his 2011 poem "Suburban Style" 郊区作风:

> in the days that remain, to endure is to look forward
> free on the weekend: up into the mountains for oxygen, picking
>   overripe fruit
> on a late sleepless night: penning doggerel to defend your rights
> even if things are not how you'd wished, beneath the north window
> the trains for baotou are still sweet

> 剩下的日子，熬着也是盼着
> 周末得空：上山吸氧，采摘熟烂瓜果
> 深夜不睡：写写打油诗维权
> 即使不能如愿，北边窗户下
> 那些开往包头的火车还是甜蜜的

One of Jiang Tao's enduring themes is change and impermanence, but perhaps especially its consequence, nostalgia. The inadequacy of the present requires the evocation of the past, sometimes in the form of a lighter-hearted youth and/or a remembered or alleged iteration of socialist China, where industrialism is colored by innocence and idealism. Huo Junming 霍俊明 in a 2014 essay described this dichotomy, to which Jiang Tao often returns, as "structuring this kind of urban truth: the present and the past, predestination and chance, routine and imagination—the vicissitudes of human life entangled in the silhouette of a late-night insomniac."

Finally, a personal note: though drawn to his wry restraint and acute concentration, I would not have ventured to translate Jiang Tao were it not for the support of the Vermont Studio Centre Henry Luce Foundation Chinese Poetry & Translation Fellowships, which paired me with him to work in residence with the poet in July 2017, in the same house as poet Xiao Kaiyu 肖開愚 and translator Christopher Lupke. As a translator of both poetry and academic works from English into Chinese, Jiang Tao provided me with crucial insights into his work and authorised some readings and choices I might not have dared to settle on without his blessing. The translations were further improved by the inspired edits and suggestions of Lucas Klein and Cris Mattison. I hope that this book, working on which has been deeply personally and intellectually rewarding for me, can help Jiang Tao's funny and ominous poetry reach a wider readership.

FOR A SPLENDID SUNNY APOCALYPSE

为一个阳光灿烂的世界末日而作

图书馆前的桃花

图书馆前的桃花注定又要开放
历尽虫蛀和赞美
仿佛一本本过期的小书
被自行车的铃声，翻到了最后一页
抬眼望去，你在窗子上
映出的脸，是比往年诚恳了一些
但树叶之间如果偶然露出
往事鲜艳的内衣
你还会逃开
满面羞惭站在10米开外？
"是谁安排了这次会面"
投币机上站立的小鸟儿
不能回答，花神忙于应酬
更不屑于回答
桃花注定开放，与此有关的知识
正在书库里轻轻澎湃

Peach Blossoms Outside the Library

peach blossoms outside the library are bound to rebloom
suffer all the insect damage and plaudits
like tiny overdue books, one after the other
thumbed to the final page by bicycle bells
lifting my eyes to watch your face
reflected in the window, a bit more candid than in days gone by
but if by chance, bygone lingerie flashes
between the leaves
would you still dash off
and stand ashamed, ten meters away?
"who arranged this meeting?"
the small bird perched on the phone booth
can't answer, nor will the god of flowers, too busy socializing,
dignify the question with a response
peach blossoms are bound to bloom, as the relevant knowledge
billows through the library stacks

郊区作风

穿体面点儿，就能像个中介了
每个早上，打开洞穴，骑电动车冲出去
人生，需要广大绿色的人脉
那随便放狗咬人的、随处开荒种菜的
人其实不坏，就想花点闲钱撒野

剩下的日子，熬着也是盼着
周末得空：上山吸氧，采摘熟烂瓜果
深夜不睡：写写打油诗维权
即使不能如愿，北边窗户下
那些开往包头的火车还是甜蜜的

甚至空了所有车厢，一整夜地
蹂躏着铁轨——惹得枕边人
也惆怅，忙不迭在被窝里
为秀气的身子，插一朵红花

Suburban Style

dress smarter, like a real estate agent
every morning, open sesame, dash out on your electric scooter
what you need in life are wide and green networks
people who sic their dogs on you, people who turn wilderness to gardens
they're not so bad, they just have a little extra cash to blow

in the days that remain, to endure is to look forward
free on the weekend: up into the mountains for oxygen, picking overripe fruit
on a late sleepless night: penning doggerel to defend your rights
even if things are not how you'd wished, beneath the north window
the trains for baotou are still sweet

even with all the cars empty, all night long
browbeating the rails—your bedfellow gets
melancholy too, worrying the blankets relentlessly so as to
thrust, into your delicate body, a red bloom.

国富论

炎炎夏日，避暑避到了西部
工人新村蔓延到小河边
家庭的暴虐、仪式
造就女孩普遍的干部作风

只有炼钢高炉还昼夜燃烧
20年前，就不为造翱翔边境的战机
只为造储备肉类的冰箱
我喜欢看男女青工一起下班

三三两两，提了青菜和肉骨头
社会理想不过是手拉手
将父母积蓄，顺便堆进浅浅的客厅
被剩下的那一个

反礼教之后，还真的无处可去了？
那么，趁天高云淡
说点什么吧，未来衣锦还乡的你！
没有通胀的当年

早恋已经普遍，无所事事的儿童
只能好高骛远地沉默
兴之所至，或到河边丢几块碎石头

The Wealth of Nations

searing summer, heading out west to escape the heat
the workers' new village sprawls to the riverside
family tyranny, ceremony
manufacturing girls all done up cadre style

only the steel blast furnaces burn night and day
twenty years ago they weren't there to make war planes to patrol the border
they just manufactured meat cold storage units
i like to watch the workers, young men and women, at shift's end

in twos and threes, carrying away greens and soup bones
a social ideal is only one hand in the other
heaping parental savings conveniently in a shallow sitting room
for the one who remains

having opposed convention, is there really nowhere left for her to go?
and yet the sky is high and the clouds sparse
so tell us a little something, you who are returning home covered in glory!
back in the day, before inflation

young love was already in vogue, and idle children
could only aim so high and maintain silence
or, when the sap rose, head down to the river to skip stones

高校一夜

究竟什么发生了改变，青山
依旧飞过了操场
校园还是划分了阴阳
所有人，还是那样在沉睡

他们睡在草叶下，睡在电话边
睡在静静的湖面和高高的水塔上
他们甚至睡在了垃圾袋里
张大的毛孔，渗出过
粗鲁的外语和罪孽的花香

十年前，他们就这样沉睡着
但所有沉睡的人，又似乎都在埋伏
用身子抵住床板，所有在埋伏中
变得吃力的人，又似乎在偷笑
都得到了暗中的好处
只能顾此失彼吗？

在蚊帐深处捕捉两只染色体
红色与绿色，蚂蚱与蜻蜓

One Night at College

but what has changed, green mountains
still soar over the sports track
campus is still bisected, yin and yang
everyone's fast asleep anyhow

they are sleeping under blades of grass, sleeping by the telephone
sleeping on the lake's still surface and high in the water tower
they even sleep in garbage bags
dilated pores exuding
crude foreign lingo and sinful floral scents

ten years ago, that's just how they slept
yet all the sleepers seemed to lie in ambush
bracing themselves against bedframes, exhausted
from lying in wait, though also possibly snickering
gaining some shadowy benefit
does managing one thing mean neglecting another?

two chromosomes are trapped in the depths of a mosquito net,
red and green, locust and dragonfly

野蹟海滩

那些看不见的岛，敲锣打鼓
不见得住着十万神仙
宴会上的螃蟹，举手举脚
投出反对票，结果拆卸之后
成了美味中的纯装置性

两个亲密的人，还可以讲民主
一起睡到空调下
大海临窗，像临窗递过一只绿色脸盆
他们梦中的脸，脏脏的
仿佛遭受过鞭打
他们身子下，流出了细沙

公路辗转，却从苍翠山巅相继送来
更多大国观光客
他们拍照、尖叫，就差在海滩上
升起一面五星旗帜
潮水适时卷走一架尼康相机

一切旖旎风光报废
几张痛苦的婚前不雅照
却被意外地保留了下来

Noseki Beach

those invisible isles, drumbeat, gongs
one hundred thousand immortals might not live there
the banquet crab raises its pincers,
votes to oppose, though once dismantled
becomes an apparatus for gourmands

two intimate people can still avow democracy
sleep together in air conditioning while
the sea reaches the window, green washbasin swirling
in dreams their faces are filthy
like they've been lashed
thin sand sifts from their bodies

highways winding through green hilltops transmit
more tourists from the great nation
taking snapshots, shrieking, all but
raising a five-star flag on the beach
the incoming tide carries off a nikon camera

the entire fluttering landscape's a write-off
though a few painfully trashy pics from before the wedding
have, quite unexpectedly, survived

夏天的回忆

穿着短裤，坐在一张照片里，山路
急转，露出苍山之颠

向下望去，闲置的房产更多了
河水环绕新发小区，奔驰车尾随马车之后

天空像是蹲了下去，又吃力地把一片云举起
为的是照顾他们打开电话

好查看妻儿的短信，却无意中看到
被山风刮走的高大身影

更多的登山者，为了减肥，才汗流浃背
吞吃药片，但最终花了38元

好在缆车上读书、亲吻
嫌社会生活不够短促

岩石边，只有你发出了蓝光
随身携带的两颗心脏，有一颗已耗尽了电能

Summer Memory

in shorts, sitting in a photo, mountain roads
swerving, disclosing green peaks

gazing beneath us, even more idle real estate
a river encircling the new development, mercedes tailgating a horsecart

the sky squats, straining to lift a cloud
so they can switch on their cell phones

to check their family chats, chancing to see
a massive shadow blown away by a mountain breeze

more hikers, sweat-drenched to lose weight
gobbling pills, but in the end dropping 38 bucks

so they can read on the chairlift and make out
carping about life in society, not brief enough

at the cliffs, only you radiate blue light
you packed two hearts, one of them's out of battery

恒春海滩

反倒是我们之中的长者，最先建议裸泳
年轻人只用抽烟的稀疏的影子附和
暗地里，他们摆弄新买的草帽
把海滩人物和飞鸟收藏进相机。

平日里，他们的表现果真动物性
在餐桌边贪吃又好辩，在异乡如在故乡
举止轻率不稳健。他们的可爱处
被长者看在眼中，喜忧参半在心上

此刻，雨点打在沙子上，打在各种印象
的相互反对与相互依恋中
仿佛万物初始，就如此乱麻一团
但60年了，海水没有真的变老

还能挺起白沫的前胸，吸引年轻一代
当然，它也没能变地更有力
能真地推开这座岛，露出下面
暗红的山口和那些牺牲掉了的水鬼。

隔着海，年轻人叫春，叫劲儿，发邮件。
我们之中终于有人下海了
他并未褪去省籍，裸露处却傲人平坦。
海水又一次次礼貌地送他轻松上岸。

At the Beach in Hengchun

but then it's the eldest who suggests skinny dipping
sparse smoke is how the young ones assent
fiddling covertly with newly bought straw hats
storing beachgoers and bird flight in their cameras

ordinarily, their behavior is simply beastly
pigging out at the dining table and arguing, at home or abroad,
indiscreet and unreliable. the eldest observes
their charm, half worried half pleased

just then, raindrops start falling on the sand, falling among
the mutual contradictions and mutual loves
apparently all things begin from such a jumble
though in sixty years the seawater hasn't really aged

squared shoulders white-frothing chest still draw the younger generation,
haven't gotten any stronger naturally
not strong enough to push away this island, or reveal the
vermilion crater, the martyred water demons beneath.

with the ocean between, the youth caterwaul, match strength, send emails.
someone has finally gone into the sea
he has not cast off his home province, though the revelation is impressively flat
the polite seawater delivers him courteously back to shore, time and again.

预言或追忆

最终，责任会被推卸给第三者
譬如角落里的国产电视机
它像一位离任后的元首
满脸深秋残忍的条纹

早餐在户外进行，伴随着鸟鸣
牛肉午餐必须搬回室内
遗留在草地上的斗争
仿佛吃剩的骨头区别于万物

踢球的孩子们，像群冒失的海鸟
追逐着泡沫，不可见的雨被一张光碟
反复播放在他们眸子里："如果"
"或许"、"然而""总之"

当词语和餐具，被洗净
放回原处，风景在塌陷的地方
仍在提出问题：或许我们的身体
是小小的邮包被误投到这里

妇产院外，条条大路通向此刻
一个素昧平生的护士
抱起了邮包，在变压器的嗡嗡声中
读出了那模糊的地址

Prophecy or Recollection

the buck will finally be passed to someone else entirely
e.g. the made-in-china tv in the corner
whose face, like an abdicated sovereign,
is scored by ruthless late-autumn streaks

breakfast proceeds outdoors with accompanying birdsong
the beef luncheon has to be brought back inside
remains of the struggle left on the grass
like a gnawed bone, something wholly apart

kicking a ball around, the kids are like a flock of rash gulls
chasing bubbles, invisible rain looping on
a cd in their pupils: "if"
"perhaps" "however" "anyhow"

when the terms and dishes are purified
and put away, the subsiding scenery
still raises questions: maybe our bodies
are tiny parcels, delivered here by mistake

from the maternity hospital each highway leads to this instant
a nurse i've never seen
hugs the package, reads out that blurry address
while the rectiformer buzzes

剧情

这个早上不会有大希奇
迟迟不来的，还有预报中的雨，
于是，某人的电视脸就打开了
差遣雷公和电母
去一个有线频道里，练曹禺的对白
剩下的新闻不用瞧
都是昨晚的旧闻
剩下的大梦还得赶着做
有今天没明天的，剧本没写完
观众席可不能老空着
当然，好天气不是肥皂剧
集体的巧合和汗液太多了
就廉价了，造作了
于是，把乌云的裙带关系
搞清楚，就告退吧
一个人躲清净，上厕所
顺手在低空的涡流里，捞起一把纸
剩3分钟
抓紧读房东未刊的处女作

The Plot

nothing will be astonishing this morning
among things yet to arrive is the forecast rain
that's why a certain someone's tv face is switched on
dispatching god of thunder and lightning deity
zap to the cable channel, they're running lines from cao yu's plays
the rest of the news isn't worth checking
reruns of last night's shows
better hurry up and dream what's left of the big dreams
it's all today, there's no tomorrow, the playwright isn't done
but the audience seats can't yawn empty forever
of course, good weather is no soap opera
the coincidences too clustered, too much sweat
in consequence it's cut-price, artificial
so: figure out the nepotism
among the storm clouds, withdraw
and hide alone, clean and quiet, go to the bathroom
and when you happen to hit the vortex of lower altitudes,
dredge up a handful of paper,
and with three minutes left,
rush to read the landlord's unpublished maiden opus.

尊重

我不尊重制度，这没关系
所有朋友都貌似一样
但我不尊重水草，不尊重自然界里
那些维系我们呼吸的机器

我在湖泊上穿着皮鞋
在城市里，学着像云一样地社交
缺少恶的取向，更缺少善的勇气
所以到了晚间，漆黑一团

我只能像刀子一样
裹紧棉被睡觉，听任身体的
尖锐处，淌出酸痛的水滴。
这世界只剩十几个平方

这冰箱里，只剩一颗会说人话的人头。
但总有好事者提早报废
好让一个觉悟的阶级，在上班时分
看上还不至过于拥挤

我不尊重少数人的牺牲
就像我不尊重刮大风
还出门工作的推销员，但我尊重
他们将一年的积蓄

像细小的尘沙，都穿在了身上
我尊重这种风格
即便我不尊重他们在乡下
有弄权的阔亲戚。

Respect

i don't respect the system, that's ok
it seems like all my friends are the same
but i don't respect seaweed, i don't respect machines
in nature that ensure our breathing

i wear leather shoes on the lake
in the city i learn to socialize like a cloud
i have no knack for evil, even less the courage to be good
so by evening it's all gone black

i can only be like a knife
wrapped tight in a quilt to sleep, obeying the body's
blade to express a raindrop of aching.
only a few square meters remain in this world

and nothing is left in the fridge but a talkative skull.
there's always busybodies tossing things out too soon
so the enlightened class can look less crowded
during the commute

i don't respect the minority's sacrifices
just like i don't respect the salespeople who
leave home in heavy winds, though i respect
the way their annual savings are worn

on the body like tiny grains of dust
there's a style i respect
even if i don't respect their newly rich cousins
in the countryside, nor their privilege.

洞中一日

现如今，住的是足够高了
仿佛伸一伸手，就能摸到
洞顶的雪（这新房
怎么看都更像一个山洞）
没有毛瑟枪，就拿把毛刷吧
涂抹壁上几道爪痕
新添的，带了一点母性。

倘若天气晴好，还能从洞口
探身出去，这京郊大地
原来有美洲风，水泥在天边
连续浇筑了框架、断面
然后，又陡峭地、插入万户
一处处的人民城郭
有黑狗在跳、在和白狗咬。

可你又在哪？一大早，好性格
又伤过人，于是粘上绿毛
蹲在半空：等了沏茶、放屁
等牛肉下锅？电钻唱歌？
再呆一会，装修的队伍
就要来了，扛了梯子、壁上观
洗剪吹的师傅也要来了

（今天换了一条新皮裤）
鸟儿问答：洞中一日，外面多少年？
看洞外，千万上班族
一大早，还是确认蝼蚁命

A Day in the Cave

living high enough now
if you stretched out your hand seems like you could touch
snow on the cave roof (this new apartment
is a lot like a cave no matter how you look at it)
no mauser, so just take a paintbrush
and smear over the wall's claw marks,
new additions that hint at motherliness.

in fine weather you can even lean from
the cave's mouth, the expanse on the capital's fringe
used to have an american tinge, cement to the horizon
being poured forever into frames, cross-sections
next, inserted precipitously into every home
in site after site of the people's cities
the black dog jumps, swaps bites with the white dog.

but where are you? early morning, a chipper personality
draws blood again, squats mid-air
gluing on green feathers: waiting for the tea to steep, for impromptu farts?
for the beef to be thrown in the wok? for the electric drill to carol?
wait a bit longer, the renovation squad's
on its way, shouldering ladders, rubbernecking over the wall
the wash-cut-and-dry barber will come too

(wearing new leather pants today)
q & a with the birds: a day in the cave—how many years is that out there?
looking outside the cave, the commuting millions
corroborate their ant-like fate in the early morning

四面八方刷屏、抄近道
比赛不团结，或咬了热煎饼
轮番升降地表

多亏了他们，江山不变色
在电视墙上，比二十年前更高清
当然，个别人士曾被辗碎
也早已从长街站起，纷纷地
步入了会场，学院
间或，还有人扮演蜘蛛侠
手腕弹出长长纤维

一下子，从北京弹落昌平
保佑这帮坏小子！
跳着的心脏不堵塞，二十年后
还像一个个黑窟窿
他们的战壕、沙发床持续
搬到了山外，也保佑山外旧区
又翻出一座新城，包括
那些费劲装修出的
寒碜的厨房、寒碜的客厅
保佑不开裂，不渗漏
正一层又一层，旋转了，垒叠得更高
垒上新山岗，垒成了擎天树
"乡下人听传奇故事
都是一笔笔的狗肉账"

山岗上的领袖，如是说
在架上行走，如是我闻：
这装修仅半日，世上未革命

ubiquitous, scrolling down screens, taking short-cuts
competing for discord, scarfing down hot pancakes
now raising, now depressing the earth's surface

is it thanks to them? rivers and mountains don't change hue
on the tv wall, higher def than twenty years back
of course, the occasional person was trampled
and long since picked themselves up from the long road, one after another
they stride into the halls, the colleges,
or else dress up like spiderman
squirt long fibers from their wrists

bounced from beijing to settle in changping
bless this pack of brats!
may the beating heart remain uncongested in twenty years
it's still like a black cavern
their trenches, their sofa beds perpetually
moved beyond the mountains, and bless
those old zones beyond the mountains
flipping again to a new city, including

those strenuously renovated
hideous kitchens, hideous living rooms
bless them so they may not crack, may not leak
and that every floor revolves, piles up higher
piles a new hill up, piles trees up to prop up heaven
"country people hear lots of legends
but know you can't make them pay"

thus spake the leader on the hill
walking on furnishings, just like i'd heard:
the renovation lasted half a day,

洞中已大变——你跌倒、爬起
抱拳，又轻跺了地板
抑或，把脑袋塞进花盆
等天下雨？等不归人？

可手机不来电也震颤
在裤子里，像一次次
不分场合地求欢、求问？

no world revolution yet
though everything's changed in the cave—you stumbled, clambered
                    up again
cupped your fist in respect, gingerly tested the boards with your feet
or stuck your head in the flowerpots
waiting for it to rain? waiting for the unreturned?

even with no incoming call your cell
vibrates in your pants, over and over
heedless of occasion, like a proposition, a query?

病后联想

奔波一整天，只为捧回这些
粉色和蓝色的小药片
它们堆在那儿，像许多的纽扣
云的纽扣、燕子的纽扣、囚徒的纽扣
从张枣的诗中纷纷地
掉了下来，从某个集中营里
被静悄悄送了出来

原来，终生志业只属于
劳动密集型
——它曾搅动江南水乡
它曾累垮过腾飞的东亚
想清楚这一点
今夏，计划沿渤海慢跑
那里开发区无人，适合独自吐纳

Convalescent Associations

hustled all day just to bring back in cupped hands these
little pink pills, blue pills
heaped like so many buttons
cloud buttons, sparrow buttons, convict buttons
falling jumbled from
zhang zao's poems, dispatched stealthily
from some concentration camp

it turns out a lifelong job is a
labor intensive model
—once it roiled the jiangnan water villages
once it made soaring east asia collapse
having worked it out
this summer, my plan is to jog 'round the bohai sea
in the open economic zone without a soul, so fit for
breathing in, breathing out, all alone

惺忪诗

你好，下午！太多的下午！
哦，这不是说西去的太阳
碾碎了更多的房东，或是我们的狗儿
在地板上发育得太慢
大楼三层以上，男孩们的骑射
早已弓身向左

而我还赤着脚，看你裸着大汗腺
站进小区草地：夕阳都已经
那样了，总得给出个理由，
解释真正——既往不咎的心
总得节约体重、胡须
在另一所房子，另一面穿衣镜前

再塑出一个自己：他的嗓音
比现在更低沉，眉目也更清晰
象黎明发亮的树梢。
他会大声说话，甚至练习诗朗诵
不在乎这个空调的世界里
早已安装了静音的森林

就这样吧，你干干净净穿着羽毛
看我戴着孔雀的镣铐
总得练习从这里，从每一分钟里
省出一秒，留给真正勇敢的一天
就象辣椒遇到了饕餮的山谷
沉睡的手臂上
涌出一根越海的电话线

Just Woke Up Poem

hey there, afternoon! so much afternoon!
ah, this is not about how the setting sun
crushes more landlords, nor how our dogs
gradually pass through puberty on our floors
above the building's third story boys practice
horsemanship, archery, bending left

and i'm still barefoot, watching you bare your sweat glands
as you venture onto the lawn: sunset already
so far gone, some reason must be given
to explain the authentic . . . the forgiving heart
must economize weight, beard
so that in another apartment, in front of a different dressing mirror

i can fashion yet another self: his voice will be
deeper than now, eyes lined and brows sharp
as treetops gleaming in the dawn.
he will speak loudly, even practice declamation
he doesn't care that this air-conditioned world
installed forests on mute

let's leave it at that, just cleanly don the feather
watch me put the peacock's shackles on
one has to practice how to save a second
out of every minute, compiling them to make a truly brave day
just like when hot peppers meet the valley of gluttony
as on our soundly sleeping arms,
the transoceanic telephone line wells up

但我还是被打翻了，言语不通
坐回同类里
（不停地换用左右脑）
看空气中，死心眼的小虫
为告别而忙碌，即使我的身体
还挨着你，就象米饭挨着菜

but i was still overthrown, we had no common language
i sat back down with my own kind
(constantly alternating between the brain's hemispheres)
watching the floating, obstinate bugs
bustling to say farewell, even if my body
is still by your side, like rice next to vegetables

歌剧见闻

像一个习惯孤独的人在晚会上浑身不适
那束玫瑰在音箱里天真地寻找百花园
而掌声从最后一排礁石传来
大海也不见得有这样的风雅：在耳朵和
暴雨之间竖起同情心的屏风
女歌手斯蒂芬或其他，我们不在乎
谁是谁的表亲，恰似你的温柔
还是把身边异性伙伴当作一只苗条的购物袋
都无关大局，投桃报李
反正每颗心灵都该伤感得象
喷洒农药后的果园
你看！幕布垂下后哭泣的身姿
早已经印在节目单上（经过了
有关方面的审核以及小鸟们的认同）
放心吧，在话筒的盲音里
主人公乏味的青春期不会拖延得太久
歌唱在不停地用抹布擦拭她的腋下
那些汗水，浸透了色情的盐
而从剧院顶棚一只壁虎危险的角度看
适才你我在后台谈论的不幸
与贵宾腰部悬垂的迷你手机相比
虽伯仲难分，但仍小巧玲珑

Opera Info

the way someone used to solitude is uncomfortable at parties
that rose in the loudspeaker innocently seeks a lush flower garden
while applause streams up from the last row of reefs
even the ocean may have no such refinements: between ear and
storm stands a sympathetic screen
josephine the singer or someone else, we don't care who's
whose cousin, just like your tenderness
may still regard the opposite sex as a graceful shopping bag
it all matters very little, trading plums for peaches
in any case each soul should be as sentimental as
an orchard after the pesticide spray
look! the weepy post-curtain-fall posture has
already been printed in the program (having
undergone relevant checks and gotten the birds' endorsement)
relax, in the dead air of the receiver
the protagonist's drab youth will not persist
singing she keeps rubbing her armpits with a rag
that sweat, suffusing the salt of eros
one may watch like a gecko from dangerous nooks of the opera ceiling
the misfortune we chatted about just now backstage
which, when compared to the phone hanging from the patroness' waist,
is as alike as can be, yet daintier and more delicate

一个作了讲师的下午

黑压压的一片，目光怎能这么轻易
就分出了类型：男与女、正与邪、昆虫和外星人
时光也从左脸放纵到右脸
停下的时候，就下课了，讲台像悬崖自动地落下

原来，这世界大得很，每一片树叶下
都藏了一对偷吻的学生，在那一泡像被尿出的但并不因此
而著名的湖上，也浮了更广大的坟

不需要准备，就可以放声，就可以变形
——时刻准备着，但据来电显示
我的变形要从鳞翅目开始，也不轻松。

One Afternoon When I Was a Lecturer

in pitch dark, how can a gaze so rashly
distinguish: men from women, righteous from evil, insects from aliens
time indulges from the left to right cheek
and when it stops, school's out, the speaker's platform sinks like a cliff

it turns out this world is enormous, hidden under every leaf
is a student couple making out on the sly, while on that pond, which looks
like someone pissed it there, though that's not why it's famous, float even
                larger tombs

no prep needed, you can raise your voice, you can morph
—but always be prepared, since according to caller ID
my metamorphosis must begin as a butterfly, and that's no joke.

教育诗

车子转过街角，就看到了她们
靴子洁白，上身隐约透出鹿纹
司机也放慢了车速，似乎心领神会
——这夜色正漫长
不妨隔了车窗，问候一下
那些花苞和枝桠的冻伤。

她们，却既不牵扯，也不搭讪
只是站在被选择的一边
单腿站在星空高大的墙下
星空也真寥廓，细长的银河外
正闲逛了几个瘦小牛郎

你感觉到了对称，于是
缩了脖子，想将套中温暖
保持到最终，但街的另一边
牛肉面馆的灯火
亮得怕人，几个新疆人

鹰鼻深目，像刚从壁画里走出的
看情形，是要将一切接管
好在这一切，都会在瞬间滑过
最后的那一个肯定
是最年少的，她弯着小腿

做出跳跃的暗示，仿佛前面
就有一片温润的草场
车灯闪烁下，你还注意到
为了浅尝这社会之黑
她甚至涂抹了一点点嫣红的骈枝

Educational Poem

as soon as the car turns the corner we see them
pure white boots, deerhide patterns dim the torso
the driver slows, almost intuitively
—night's endless glow
why not send greetings across the window
to the frost that harms the buds and twigs

as for them, they don't intrude, don't chat
simply stand on their chosen side
on one foot under heaven's high and starry wall
the stars are so vast, beyond the meagre milky way
a few skinny cowherds mosey

you sense the symmetry, so you
draw in your neck, wanting to keep warmth sheathed
to the end, but at the other end of the street
the beef noodle joint's lights are scary
bright, and a few people from xinjiang

eagle-nosed, sunken-eyed, like they stepped from a wall painting
it depends, you may have to take over everything
at least that will all slide away in an instant
the last of them is definitely
the youngest, she flexes her leg

hints at a leap, as though up ahead
there was some moist pasture
the car lights flicker once you realize that
in order to dabble in society's darkness
she has even applied a touch of red to a sixth finger

少壮派报告

坦白总是好作风，没有教官同睡
在床上也得直挺挺
何况来你我自小地方
父母经营家族商社，倒卖近海鱼鲜

在落花的高等学府
课业本无常，人生却总有水平线。
跟了前辈，朝九晚五地飞吧
那些美妙的神经质的事情
求之不得，又总使人心思烦乱

终有一天，论文的草稿里
会扑棱棱跃起一大群野鸭子
或呼啦啦地站起一大群猛男
他们一批批地出征
曾腐烂在了亚洲腹地

穿着考究的时候
就拿自己当了局外人
纷纷行走在AV片中的外景空间

Report on the Up-and-Comers

frankness is always the best policy, even if the cadet officer's not sleeping
in the same room we must still lie at attention in our beds
especially since you and i are both small town boys
from mom and pop shops selling overpriced seafood from the coast

in higher learning's fallen flower
the class workload varies, but life is benchmarked.
so go flying with the older generation from nine to five
those matters of marvelous neurosis
are all we have to wish for, and always perturbing

finally one day, in the article's draft
will swoosh a great flock of wild ducks
or thumpity-thump a great flock of thugs will rise
one after the other setting out to war
once they rotted in asia's gut

when meticulously dressed
selves seem to be outsiders
each strolling through an exterior porno shoot

罪中罪

沿着花墙，是风—节节
数着自己的喉结，猫的叫声
则污染了春夜的一角。

但此刻，月光还是卫生的
我们在小区里溜达，追忆
六年前的初遇：喜鹊在枝头

铺设电线，一座矿业学院
陷入女生梦里的胡话。
两只手不安地对谈，试着掏出

树林乳沟中的天籁
人如月，天如纸，星斗如孝子伏床
只是操场独自个翻了个身

让冰凉的看台压在唇上
——新吻，迷失了旧方向。
你说：神是救主，我不予否认

只补充若干细节：浮云、护膝
暖腰的水袋，但万物稀稀
疏疏，象动物归巢，都掩映到

相拥的身上，连枝桠间
如此矛盾的等式，也撑起人形
竟被我们愚蠢地证明过了。

Sin among Sins

along the wall of flowers, gust after
gust counts its own adam's apples, though a cat's call
has polluted one spring night's cranny.

but for the nonce, moonlight remains hygienic
we stroll the neighborhood, recollecting
when first we met, six years ago: a magpie on a branch

arranging wires, an institute of mining technology
mired in the gibberish of some girlish dream.
two hands converse uneasily, trying to fish

heaven free, stuck in the forest's cleavage
people are lunar, the sky papery, the stars filial sons at sickbed
it's just the sportsground tossing and turning

trapping an icy grandstand beneath my lips
—a new kiss, misplacing old directions.
you say: god saves, and i can't deny it

but i add a flourish or two: floating clouds, kneepads
hot water bottles for a sore back, all things are few
and far between, like homing animals, all casting shadows

over embracing flesh, and even the contradictions
of the branching foliage, propping up the human form
turn out to be equations we have idiotically proven.

梦中婚礼

一堆人吵吵嚷嚷的，将一座动物园
搬进了室内：假山果真是假的
还有喷泉在喷水，让客厅
尽量显出天然的气派

大舅哥是山东人，一缕湿发
粘住多肉的大脑壳，他的朋友
来自德国，用手比划着对称的感伤
他告诉你：自己名叫"巴特"。

但事情远未开始，鱼贯而入的声音
让你发现其实是站在一座天桥上
俯瞰假日柔嫩的深渊：
客人环坐喷烟，纷纷剥开糖纸

捧出玲珑的心。还有外甥和狗
在腿边环绕，大脑壳象家族的徽章
醒目异常。大舅哥无意中吐露
他们的名字：也是"巴特"

只有新娘还未出现，她必然渊博、巧智
深知其中的奥秘．于是黝黑的脸
于相框里一点点蒸发、消散。一阵风刮过
架上所有的瓷器，都点头称是

多少有点残酷的是，没有人
继续发现你，花园衬托着你的孤寂
地毯张开嘲讽的小嘴——捧着肉锅的伴郎

Wedding in the Dream

a pack of noisy people, a zoo transplanted
indoors: the fake mountain is a real fake
also the water fountain fountaining water, making the living
room as impressively natural as possible

uncle from shandong, one strand of moist hair
glued to his big fleshy dome, his friend comes
from germany and with gestures of symmetrical melancholy
tells you: his name is "barth."

but things are not yet underway, successive noises
reveal you to be standing under a skyway
overlooking the tender depths of the holiday
the guests sit in a circle spouting smoke, unwrapping individual candies

to extract the delicate hearts. not to mention nephew and dog
circling underfoot, the big noggin, like a family badge,
sticking out like a sore thumb. uncle has unwittingly divulged
their names: also "barth."

only the bride has not yet emerged, inevitably erudite, astonishingly wise
profound possessor of this arcana. so swarthy faces
disperse bit by bit from the photo frames, evaporate. a gust of wind passes
the ceramics in the case nod affirmation.

what's cruel to some degree is that no one
keeps discovering you, the garden sets off your solitude
the carpet opens its sarcastic little mouth—the best man carrying the meat-pot

象个伪神，被搏挤在最外边
窗外，夏天提早到来，万木葱茏
阻挡了太阳的噪音，从敞开的门缝，
你还瞥见，内室里的岳父拉着岳母
像背阴的泰山和华山，正在衣橱边悄声低语

is, like a false god, wrestled to the furthest reaches
outside the window, the summer is premature, its green lushness
blocking the sun's din, the door is open a crack
glimpsing the inner room you see father-in-law tugging mother-in-law close
like two hulking mountains in shadows, whispering low by the dresser

内心的苇草

首先声明的是，这些只是"话"
不能在小贩手里批发，也不能听凭
记忆里伸出的镊子
一根根，从风景的鬓毛中拔取

朝九晚五，大家都是这样
吹牛，抓阄，把"话"凌空抛撒
说不出的和不想说出的
彼此只是甲和乙，A和B

无论输多赢少，不要太紧张
一切只发生在一首诗里。
就象这个下午，头插黑暗的翎花
我端坐着，羽翼丰满

即便睡着了，怀里的江和海
也会自动翻滚，淹了一亩新客厅
但此时，有人扭亮台灯
让我从沙发里，不断地裸露出来

象一个古代的日本人
皮肤皱紫，眼袋含着阴影
我惊讶地坦白：自己曾复姓"田野"
只是为了让某人自夸为"镰刀"

Heart Reeds

the first thing to state is that all this is just "talk"
it cannot be wholesaled by a peddler nor can it permit
tweezers which protrude from memory to
yank it hair by hair from scenery's sideburns

from nine to five, everybody is
shooting the shit, drawing lots, pitching "talk" high in the air
things you can't say and things you don't want to say
are alpha and beta, a and b to each other

no matter what you win or lose, don't be nervous
everything is only happening in a poem.
just like this afternoon, my head plumed with darkness
i sat erect, with fulsome wings

though asleep, the river and sea of my embrace
will churn automatically and flood the ten-acre new living room
but this time someone dialed up the desk lamp
exposing me eternally on the sofa

like a japanese man from ancient times
with densely wrinkled skin, shadowy eyebags
i confess in surprise: i gave myself the name Tano, meaning field
only so that a certain someone would esteem themselves Sickle

家庭计划

青山不会自己吐血
当然也不会主动跳上桌子
成为我们之间的一副骨牌
本来，计划妥当
在分叉的经济中，抽出一根枯枝
抽打这个下午暴露的臀部

但你说，要向生活的强者看齐
要向身边两万元的密友看齐：
他们的西装上布满血管和青筋
他们的方阵，已逼近了厨房

于是，天空的颜色变了，
窗外的小园收缩到了一枚葱的袜跟里
我们彼此修改了脸形
面对面坐着，牌也摊开了
等待谁先主动
解开了弱者的扣子

Family Plans

the green hills won't spit blood on their own
or leap on the table of their own accord
to become a domino between us
to begin with we had a reasonable plan
in a bifurcated economy, extracting a dry twig
to spank these buttocks exposed in the afternoon

but you say one must fall into the line life dictates
the line set by your twenty-thousand-dollar closest friends
their suits spangled with blood vessels and blue veins
their phalanx already nearing the kitchen

hence, the sky's color changes
the garden outside the window shrinks into the heel of a scallion's sock
we have each corrected the shape of the other's face
sitting eye-to-eye, cards on the table
waiting to see who will first
undo the weaker's buttons

即景

又是一年草木葱茏，天色氤氲
我站在阳台上，看小区警卫
三三俩俩把守疫情和道路
尘土扬起，在阳光下抖动金色衣袂
狗儿吠叫，好让一身筋骨发育在痒处。

我不理解气味，不理解主妇嘴里为什么
突然冒出了东北话，不理解肌肉里那些纤维状的山麓
其实我不理解的还有很多
它们层叠着、晦涩着、在春光里充斥着
正等待一个知识分子沉溺于收集。

他和我一样，站在六层的高度、危情的高度
重新将各种各样植物的族谱默念
只有一点不同，他穿着高领毛衣，露出喉结和头颅
而我的圆领衫久经漂洗：又是一年
春光涣散，勾出男人的胸乳

Visual Inspiration

one more year of lush grass, dusk envelops
me standing on the balcony, looking down at neighborhood security
in twos and threes guarding the epidemic situation and the roads
dust rises, the golden apparel trembles in the sun
a dog barks, his body maturing where he longs to scratch

i don't get smell, i don't get why housewives' mouths need
to suddenly burst out in a northeastern burr, i don't get those reticular foothills
actually there's lots of other things i don't get
layered, cryptic, congested in spring light
waiting for an intellectual to wallow in collection.

he's like me, lofty on the sixth floor, altitude's a risk
silently repeating a genealogy for plants
with one difference, his turtleneck unpeels adam's apple and skull
while my crew-neck has long been through the laundry: one more year
the spring brilliance slackens, outlining a male breast

冬至日

比棋局还要漫长，白色迫近
一条林荫路摘光了脚踝
太阳走着的地方，没人轻易靠近
但似乎还有力气，迈出这一步
在十一月换上夏天的短袖衫
自己咽下腥红的喉——不让它发热
在夜间变得更为迫切，因为
看不见的瀑布，时刻倾泻着我们
与世界对坐的另一群人
喝完了啤酒，也总会起身
或在黑暗的地基中，坐着观天
把头顶的瓦砾一片片挪开

Winter Solstice

for even longer than a game of chess, white approaches
the tree-shaded road that's culled all the ankles
where the sun paces, no one rashly comes near
but they still seem to have the energy to take this step
changing into summer short-sleeve shirts in november
swallowing a scarlet throat—it mustn't grow feverish
or urgent overnight, on account of
the unseen waterfall, always rushing down upon us and
the other people, sitting face-to-face with the world
who have finished their beer, and will always rise
or sit and, in the dark foundation, watch the sky
as they clear away the rubble from over their heads

卜居

体力准确地由星座测试
鼻翼间的小小风暴，淹没了鲁滨逊
俊俏的船尾，而你还来不及
将十指削成铅笔，一座农业专科学校
却已被排挤到城市边缘
在游泳池、小松林、老年合唱团之间
你只得摆下一张书桌
像启蒙学者在历史和战乱间选择了
一个形容词——当然要轻松得多
不那么悲壮，不那么戏剧感
黎明，会有卡车从运来方便面
萝卜干和鲜牛奶，正午时喜鹊走入内室
脱下连衣裙，变身麻雀飞出
到了黄昏或午夜，你尾随一位打电话的少女
到小杂货铺去买烟
听到老板闲话，豁开了近代史的嘴唇

Divining the Dwelling

vigor accurately zodiac-gauged
a tiny squall between the nose flaps submerges robinson crusoe's
elegant stern, and still there isn't time
to sharpen your ten fingers to pencils, though a farming college
already squeezes into the city outskirts
between the swimming pool, the stand of pine, and the seniors' choir
you need only set up a writing desk
like the enlightenment thinkers, choosing one adjective
between history and war—naturally we have to be much chiller
not so tragic, not so theatrical
at dawn, the truck will deliver instant noodles dried radishes
and fresh milk, at noon the magpie walks into the inner chamber
to remove its one-piece, turns into a sparrow and flies away
at dusk or midnight, you trail a telephoning teenage girl
to the corner store to buy smokes
hearing the owner gossip, modern history's lips cleave

重逢

两个友人坐进电视里
神色有点慌张，肯定是顾及到了
电视机外我的存在
其实，我不过是坐在一眼
焦黑的井里，连晚饭
还没吃上一口，还有大笔的
房租要缴，根本不想等待一个时机
悄悄爬出来

他们太多心了
连头发也染成了秋天的颜色
生怕不被我误认为树
在手里，还一直攥着黑暗的土
以为那就是见证
曾纠缠过、生长过、又被揉成一团
丢进地幔的抽屉里

但他们还是开口了
说起学生时代，多么矫情、灿烂
在睡梦里都有一队队少女
坦克般碾过
似乎只有外星人，没有在轻薄之后被遗弃
如今，大家成功了
还时不时回去漫步
为了尊重旧日青草地
高级吉普，停在远处深深的林荫里

Reunion

two friends took a seat in the television
looking a bit frazzled, must be because they were mindful of
my existence outside the tv set
actually, i was just sitting in a
char-black well, hadn't had a bite
of dinner yet, plus the enormous rent i still
have to pay, i wasn't even on the lookout for a chance
to climb out on the sly

they're overthinking it
they even dyed their hair the color of fall
lest i don't mistake them for trees
in their hands, all along, clutching dark soil
thinking it's proof
which, once corrected, has grown, rounded
to be thrown into a drawer of the earth's mantle

and yet they open their mouths
speak of student days, how opinionated, how magnificent
in their dreams, squadrons of girls always
crushing them like tanks
it seems like anyone but an alien is abandoned after the fling
now everyone's a success
even going back to ramble
out of respect over the green lawns of yore
a high-end jeep parked in the distance, in the deep shade of the forest

说到这里，他们交换了抱歉的眼神
显然在迎合我此刻的心境
我的眼里，也当真
布满粘稠的泥浆
因为在井底，我抽烟、喝茶、打字
甚至挖出过一具吉他的遗骸
但从没想起过他们
一次也没有

having said that much, they exchange apologetic glances
evidently humoring my momentary frame of mind
and my eyes truly
fill with a viscous slurry
because at the bottom of the well, i smoke, drink, type
i've even dug up the skeleton of a guitar
and the thought of those people has never occurred to me
not even once

天涯

有谁能把我带出十月
不动声色，如同带走一团
肮脏的红色。太阳是个斑点
劳动让人柔软
请把音量调小，当肉体
被啃光，齿痕留在了余粮上
谁会把剩下的形式带走
像带走一小把火柴的梗
焦黑的、没烧完的
在郊外的公路上，看小鸟
不断在补充燃料
不断吃阿司匹林
这是怎样的幸运，医治
是无效的，唱歌是费劲的
谁又将"天涯"
像一匹白马，萧萧叫着
牵离了我身边

To the Ends of the Earth

who can take me from october
maintaining composure, the way a filthy
red is excised. the sun is a speckle
labor softens people
please turn the music down, even when the flesh
has been gnawed clean, there are teeth marks on the leftovers
who will take away what's left of form
like removing a used match
charred, though not fully burnt
on the outskirt's streets, looking at birds
constantly replenishing fuel
constantly gulping aspirin
some luck, medical treatment
is ineffective, singing is strenuous
and who will lead "to the ends of the earth"
like a white horse, neighing,
away from me

菩提树下

此刻，你不是那个登台朗诵的你
用低沉的亚洲嗓音，吹凉瞌睡的山谷们
（被一盏盏阅读灯照亮的）
我也不是那个焦虑的我：一边在镜子前
服药，一边构思：五分钟后
依旧紧锁的五官

菩提本无树，在这里
本是一条大街，且早早躺了下来。
曾在友人的诗中读到过
因不了解而着迷，因着迷而自学
不断折返同一个傍晚
此刻，却冒了同样的雨

在橱窗上，看到一切都匆匆的、潦草的
那个自学的自我可能对自己
从来都够不耐心。再看满街的大男孩
不像去购物，倒像兴冲冲游行
那闲情，惟有试穿了新衣的皇帝
方能体验

但此刻，和你共用一个身子的皇帝
肯定也瞌睡了，别无用心；
我也不再疑心是否还有第三者
光了膀子同行。
拎上纸袋子，我们决定
雨中疾走，老老实实扮演购物狂

Beneath the Bodhi Tree

right now you're no longer the you reciting onstage
with your deep asian voice, breathing cool air on the dozing valleys
(illuminated by one reading lamp after another)
nor am i that overanxious me: popping pills in front
of the mirror as i consider: the sensory organs
that will still be scowling in five minutes

bodhi has no tree, and a big road
was here, though it has long since lain down.
i read that once in a friend's poem
i didn't understand and it charmed me, and the charm made me an autodidact
always turning back to this same late afternoon,
though we brave the same rain

in the kitchen window, seeing everything rushed, sloppy,
that autodidactic self has likely never shown itself
the necessary patience. again gazing at the old boys on the street
they don't look like they're shopping, they look like they're on some
                    giddy demo
a leisureliness only an emperor trying on new clothes
can truly experience

but right now, the emperor who shares your body
is surely dozing, you'll need to be attentive;
nor do i suspect another person
might walk bare-chested alongside us.
we were accorded paper bags and decided
to rush on in the rain, making a sincere show of shopaholism

先去大众鞋城，买登山鞋
你选的一双，尺码超大，鞋底有轮胎花纹
像是直接从斯大林格勒的战场
一路走回来的
在隔壁，我试穿的上衣
中规中矩，只在领子里
藏了一只扁扁的雨神的风帽

这个城市已准备好了镜头
准备好金色的小麦啤酒
似乎也准备，为大多数的事抱歉
无论坐在spree河边，还是站在河面上
都感觉有掌声从背后传来

经久不息却蛮横地，像诗中的小雨点
从酒吧、从墓地，从黑白照片
从深闷的犹太庭院
为女士拍照时，我猜想
那些拆了的墙，其实在努力建起啊

包括刻了死者名字的石头
齿轮一样从青草中冒出
让人恍然，那些夜间疾驰长街的坦克
其实也曾这样被活埋过的

first the shoe emporium, we buy some hiking boots
the pair you picked was way too big, the soles had tire treads
like they had walked straight
from the battle of stalingrad
next door i try on a jacket,
standard issue, except that within the collar
is concealed the rain god's little hood

this city is ready for its close-up
ready for a golden wheat beer
it also seems ready to apologize for most things
whether you're sitting by the spree or standing on the river's surface
it always feels like the sound of applause is behind you

prolonged but peremptory, like tiny raindrops in a poem
from the bars, the cemeteries, the black-and-white photos
from the grand jewish home with a courtyard
taking a lady's picture, i guessed that
these demolished walls were trying hard to be built

including the stones with the names of the dead carved upon them
like gears poking out of the grass
a flash of obscure understanding: those tanks speeding down long roads
                    at night
were in fact buried alive in just the same way

乡治人

水里游着电动鱼，但没有大蒜
和绿豆，在天上整齐地飞
一行人简单入住、吃茶
对了镜子，翻译各自心里话。

窗外的水乡，几乎如画
桥上行走的便衣，几乎都是
新四军后人——他们打工与否
算不上重点，家事狼藉一片

只要控制了农药。下一步
是花高价，从敌国买回锦绣工艺
那被掳去后又发达了的姊妹
果真能为此，坐了小巴

谦虚返乡？像犯下了心脏病
来访者突然卧倒，原地
去细查一颗水稻：它绿油油的身世里
有耐药小虫奔走担保

终于，饭后长谈触及社会根本
间或提到若干大省首脑
有人层峦叠嶂地躺到床里
自动加息，那一角漫漶中的韬晦

Village Administrator

robot fish swim in the water, though no garlic
or green beans flock uniformly across the sky
the travelling party checks in, has tea,
faces the mirrors, each translating their interior monologue.

river village out the window, almost like a painting
mufti on the bridge, nearly all
descendants of the new fourth army—whether they're at work
isn't the main thing, family matters might be a mess

but the pesticides are under control. next step
is to splurge on embroidery bought back from the enemy
and that sister who was dragged off and made it big
might actually travel modestly, in a

minibus? as though by coronary
the visitor suddenly drops on the spot, scrutinizing
a grain of rice: its lush green life history
guaranteed by the flitting pesticide-resistant bugs

finally, long postprandial talks bear on the social foundations
occasionally dropping the names of some big provincial leaders
someone lies down on the bed like mountain ranges
interest automatically increasing, while that corner's low profile blurs

排遣

正午阳光免费按摩公园小丘
四周散落的家庭缺乏一定格式
即将出国的男士弓腰撅臀
用取景框筛选未来追忆的现场
贫家女孩儿神色匆匆走过
还未换下她厚厚的条绒冬装
情侣们抱在情深处，小口地
交换了肺中的叶绿素，宠物狗
扬起的造作小脸被轻风
传真到了远方"多漂亮的男孩"
新生儿必定是目光的焦点
像一枚稚嫩鼠标，时刻改变
父母的蓝图：事业平稳的渐进线
年龄松散的虚线，工休日展开
唇角妩媚的双曲线……
当暖湿气流在他们脸上刻下
一条均匀螺旋线，抬头仰望
天空已如胶皮轮日久年深地
绽开，唯一不能忽略的仍是
四年前吹入眼眶的那一粒尘沙

Killing Time

the high noon sun gives the hill in the park a free massage
scattered families without fixed formatting
the man about to go abroad bends like he's twerking
he uses the viewfinder to select scenes for future memory
the girl from a poor family with a harried look passes
still hasn't put away her winter corduroy jacket
lovers embrace in love's depths, with small sips
exchanging the chlorophyll in their lungs, the pet dog
raises its tiny artificial face to be
faxed into the distance by the breeze "what a strapping boy"
newborns are the eye's inevitable focal point
like a tender young computer mouse, all the time altering
the parental blueprint: smooth undertakings towards the asymptote
the dotted line of loosening age, the public holiday spreading
the gorgeous lips of its hyperbola . . .
when warm humidity has etched
an evenly helical line on their faces, heads lift to see how
as eternity passes the sky like a rubber ball
rips open, the only incontrovertible point
that grain of dust blown four years ago into the rim of the eye

为一个阳光灿烂的世界末日而作

四月十六日，阳光灿烂，微风和煦
报纸头版对此只字未提
数钞机在歌唱，木马奔驰原地
"有个人将复活，将世界带入烈火"
退休主任没吃早餐，有点失望
他的健身计划，还得继续

到了中午，气温在上升，深深的失望
更难以掩饰，告别的情侣
又在肯德基里相逢，举了火炬甜筒
银行里走出的中年人
踩了发软的柏油，一下子感觉
自己是受伤斑马
不得不坐出租车，重返食肉森林

四月十六日，春光明媚，没有烈火
没人复生，即使是死者
也放弃了期待，从地下的管道中
纷纷走散。如果侧耳倾听
收音机的长短波段上
留下了一连串微小的雪崩

"下一站，将抵达哪里"
孩子们涌入地铁，像晶莹的雪
又将被黑暗取走，四月十六日
万物恒常，各得其所

Written for a Splendid Sunny Apocalypse

april 16, it's splendid and sunny, a pleasant breeze
no mention of that in the newspaper headlines
the money counting machines sing, the trojan horse rushes back into position
"someone has brought resurrection, has brought the world into the inferno"
the retired director has not eaten breakfast, he's crestfallen
he'll just have to continue with his bodybuilding routine

at noon the temperature is rising, bitter disappointment
grows even harder to disguise, lovers bid farewell then
run into each other at KFC, lift their ice-cream cone torches
the middle-aged guy exits the bank
treads on the softening asphalt feeling
suddenly like a wounded zebra
needing a cab to return to the carnivorous forest

on april 16, a radiant spring day, no infernos,
no resurrection, even the dead
relinquish their expectations and disperse through
the underground pipes. listen closely and you'll
hear a chain of miniscule avalanches
over the radio's long or shortwave bands

"next stop, who knows where"
children pour into the subway like snow crystals,
only to be borne away by the dark, on april 16
all things are constant, each in its proper place,

彼此心照不宣
但你心里，似乎在惦记什么

为此，还买了一瓶甜酒
并匆匆跑上了居民楼的六层

with mutual though tacit understanding,
yet something is on your mind it seems

that's why i bought a bottle of sweet wine
and rushed up to the sixth floor apartment

浴室

这样被忽略，彼此间
敌视的距离，那些赤裸的上身
像橄榄树被海岸出卖
而下身无物，暴露的圣器
在反复冲洗的礼拜六
疲倦地不能扬起
人人都在默念一个词
嘴唇上衔一个空旷的浴房
雨在其中下着，世界的臀部
缓缓挪移于窗外
寻找一种关联吗？横在喷头
与云朵之间，站在热水中
站在泡沫飞溅的集体中
你脚下也横了铁索
你要到滚热的江水对面去

The Bath

to be ignored like this, between them
the distance of hostility, those naked tops
like olive trees betrayed by the shore
and nothing below the waist, the bared holy organ
on this saturday of constant washing
too fatigued to rise
everyone silently reciting a single word
the lips harboring a spacious bathing chamber
the rain falls in, the world's rump
slowly shifts outside the window
looking for some connection? horizontal
between the shower nozzle
and clouds, standing in hot water
standing in a complex of soaring foam
underfoot, the iron chain link lies crosswise
you need to cross the boiling river to the other side

久病初愈的下午

不需要阳光的手指来拨弄
这悬在脑后的一串铜铃，深秋
即使再素朴，也像一篇草就的讲稿
有那么多不必要的修辞
沉吟或眺望，不同的姿态
都印证了远方的经验
可能会重新刊印：场景、基调
反复申诉的不必要的主题

久病初愈的下午，再度想象
一片叶子，如何吮净天空的墨迹
像无知海绵，再作一次跳跃
从颤动的枝头到一个儿童
路过的、纯真的头顶
这落差让人浮想联翩吗？

而下午三时，红色围巾，作为
不速之客的小姐，请问：
在床头，在操场，在一架双杠上
看不见的燕子该如何完成
她们的排比练习？作为一个答案

一个鬼魅会手执钢叉
随时间水浪而现出原型和嘴脸。

One Afternoon When I Was Beginning to Feel Better after a Long Illness

i don't need sunny fingers sounding
the little copper bells behind my head, deep autumn
no matter how simple, is still like a lecture draft
with its superfluous rhetorical flourishes
muttering and high pitches, various postures
all corroborating the distant experience
that will perhaps be reprinted: the scenes, the fundamental key,
constantly appealing to an unnecessary subject

one afternoon when i was beginning to feel better after a long illness, i
thought of
a leaf, how it sucks the inkblots clean from the heavens
like an ignorant sponge, leaping once more
from trembling twig to a
passing child's innocent head
is it this gap that overcrowds the imagination?

but at 3 pm, with red scarf, i ask this
uninvited guest, a girl:
at the head of the bed, on the athletic field, on the parallel bars
how should invisible sparrows complete
their parallel routines? as a reply,

a demonic executioner, clutching a steel pitchfork
may, as time billows on, recover his archetype, his grinning mug.

夜行的事物

有人声称，擦去树叶上的灰尘
叶子本是梳妆镜
这镜子本无光，拒绝反射
暗绿的花纹，就是一枚枚图章
私刻了出身

所以，他们从四外飞来
沿了铁路、桥洞、未完工的巨梁
时起时落的，还有沿途
那些臭烘烘的野味儿
他们曾在水库上，蘸水洗脸
或戴了安全帽

被分成若干小组，泥泞了身子
在讨论中，脸贴脸
他们的悄悄话多半是真的
被存进了手机
被发送在星空和民族性里
被肿痛的小脑
连夜下载

可这五环以外，有点像溃乱的欧洲
黑魆魆的一片片
都是古堡、小镇、要塞
他们飞过时，我似乎听到了
引擎轻轻的轰鸣
听到了起重臂的落下

Things That Travel by Night

some claim that if you rub dust from a leaf
you'll find out the leaf was a dressing mirror
this mirror has no shine, it rejects reflection
dark green veins, like seal after engraved seal
secretly etching out what you came from

that's why they fly here from all around
along the railroad tracks, bridge arches, great unfinished beams
rising and falling, also along the
rank stench of wild things,
once at the reservoir they dipped their faces to wash
or maybe wore hardhats

split into several small groups, their bodies mired
in conversation, face stuck to face
their sweet nothings mostly real
and saved on their cell phones
delivered to the starry sky or ethnic essence
the swollen cerebellum
downloads them all night

but outside the five ring roads, it's like europe in collapse
darkness after sheet of darkness
all those castles, towns, fortresses
as they soar past i hear
the faint engine's roar
hear the lowering of the crane's boom

也闻到大气芬芳
仿佛喷洒了便宜的清新剂
你说那是雾霾再起？
不是的，不是
地火在涌动
在不远处，温热了金隅花园

草丛与砖缝里，即将灯火通明
有人摩擦两股
即将说出漂亮的京白。

and smell the atmosphere
like it's been sprayed with cheap air freshener
you say that's the smog lifting?
no, not that
it's magma surging
not so far away, warming *jinyu* gardens

grass in the brick rifts, the lights about to blaze
someone rubbing their legs together
about to speak with a lovely beijing twang.

黎明时的悔悟

黎明的雨，由具体到抽象地下着
雨里的街区也像一盘棋
由晦涩逐渐明朗。小饭铺里
早起的新疆人串起羊肉
鲜红的组织，你掌中安宁的国度
也将一个个被唤醒
这是梳头的时刻，是刀子和叉子
把什么平分了的时刻
是一支钢笔，将大海用得一滴不剩的时刻
名字叫"亚茹"的少女睡在你身边
这是她故乡的葵花
在发电厂外感到羞耻的时刻
她的鼾声时断时续
使卧室也像一艘潜水艇
在昏暗中游动，在梦中
她可能碰到了桌角，痛苦呻吟
也可能想起未交的学费、房费
"为难的事情，总是还有很多"
这与飞逝的雁群无关
与远方港口响起的汽笛无关
在那里，一个写诗的兄弟
已升任工程总监，可还是忧心忡忡
在海滩上读北京的来信
就这样，黎明的细雨，由具体
到抽象地下着，名字叫"亚茹"的少女
伸展双臂，脸上格言体的忧伤
绰约动人——"我们被抛入
像豆子进锅，还是像牛奶

Remorse at Dawn

dawn rain falling from the specific to the abstract
a city block in rain like a chessboard
progressively shaded from cryptic to obvious. in the little eatery
the early-rising xinjiang guy skewers the mutton's
scarlet tissue, the quiet nations of your palm
will also be woken, one after the other
this is the time to comb, the time for knives and forks
to divide things in equitable fashion
time for a pen to exhaust ocean's last drop
time for a girl called "yaru" to sleep at your side
time for a sunflower from her hometown
to feel ashamed outside the power station
sometimes her snoring continues sometimes it breaks off
making the bedroom seem like a submarine
roving the darkness, in her dream
she might smash into the table corner, groan painfully
or maybe recall her unpaid tuition, her rent
"greater embarrassment always lies ahead"
this has nothing to do with the wild geese who have flown away
nothing to do with the steam whistle sounding at the distant port
where there is a brother in poetry,
he's been promoted to project supervisor but he's still worried
on the beach he reads a letter from beijing
that's all, a dawn drizzle falling from
the specific to the abstract, a girl called "yaru"
stretches out her arms, on her face sorrow like an axiom
graceful and moving—"we're for it
like beans chucked into a pan, or is it like milk

被冲入速溶咖啡？"当命运粗钝的一端
尚有一滴雨梦到倾角的优美
街口两个互致问候的出租司机
脸上不约而同，都挂了一层
朦胧的晨光与血腥

poured into instant coffee?" while the blunt end of fate
features one raindrop dreaming of the beautiful slope
at the crossing two cabbies exchange greetings
their faces coincide, both glazed with
soft morning light and blood

官司

批判两个赤膊的北京人
不等于，就支持了那个外地人
地上的脏东西证明
至少有三个人，共同污染了京郊
留下证言的一群，却不见了
曾几何时，他们穿着拖鞋
在小区门口使劲地吐痰
咳嗽的声音，甚至传到了昌平县
结果，在一个深夜
车声隆隆，他们被注销了户籍
像挖出的废土，被运得更远
譬如：在八达岭以外，在那里
皓月，虽然当空，但不支持
所有的原告和被告
连轻浮的石头，也告别荒野
擅自睡在了客厅

Suing

a critique of two half-naked beijingers
does not entail support for outsiders
besides the filth on the ground proves
there were at least three of them polluting the outskirts
the crowd that stayed behind to testify is nowhere to be found
but not so long ago, they were wearing flip-flops
and spitting with all their might at the community gates
the sound of their coughing carried all the way to changping county
the upshot was that late one night
in the rumble of cars, their household registrations were cancelled
like excavated rubble, shipped farther off
for instance: there's a bright moon beyond the great wall at badaling,
which though high overhead, supports
neither plaintiffs nor defendants and
even the stones with their levity have bid the wilderness farewell
and presume to sleep in the parlor

高峰

没奈何，这预料中的前戏
乏味又短暂，一场新雪
在我们身上，还没深深浸润过
还没真的兴奋过，乌云
就被拆走了床垫
露出的豪宅，不过是小户鸽笼
敞开向余生

好在，约定的时间未到
可以先驻足参观：树梢上
挂着冻红的果实
草地下，埋了游泳的会馆
这社区风物，竟如此熟悉
像被一一梦到过
甚至像被快乐地多次享用过

你却说：其实是眼球的凸面
沾了水汽，从B2到B3
只有向下挖掘，财富
才露出它的核心
我咕哝了几句，尝试另一种
反驳：其实只有贫穷
才俗气地讳莫如深

话不投机，还是一起攀登吧
扮演牵手的夫妇，在裸体楼梯上
辨别飘忽的陌生人：
你看，那疲倦的运水夫

Summit

it's hopeless, this expected foreplay
brief and insipid, new snowfall
on our bodies, though not yet permeating
not yet truly excited, the storm clouds
have had their mattresses ripped off
revealing a mansion which is only a humble dovecote
opening towards the rest of life

at least the appointed hour has not yet come
we can take a break, have a gander: treetops
hang with frost-red fruit
beneath the lawn, the swimming club is buried
this neighborhood's scenery is so familiar
like each detail has been dreamt
even gleefully and repeatedly enjoyed

though you say: actually it's because the eyeball's convexity is
vapor-moistened, and to get from B2 to B3
you have to keep digging down, that's where wealth
betrays its core
i mutter a few sentences, try some other
refutation: in fact only poverty
has the vulgarity to be tight-lipped

we talk at cross purposes, we'll clamber up instead
play the roles of a hand-holding couple on the stripped steps
picking out the swift strangers:
look, that exhausted water-carrier

肩扛了一大桶郊外的湖
那眉毛高挑的快递员
唇上还卖弄一抹油腻的远山
那压碎了小指的修锁匠
只能靠拇指工作，拨开树叶下的弹簧
那瞌睡的、来自安徽的小保姆
则惦记起老鳏夫
和他升天的哈巴犬

跟我们一起攀登吧，陌生人
这高楼不过十几层
这快感不过十几重
什么吵吵嚷嚷、花花草草
全是心头未了的贷款
（我们都是过来人）
可有谁没能按月地偿清？

但在那里，一切的峰巅
北风也曾强劲地狡辩
我们按下门铃，说明来意
却意外地发现：大卧室
套着小客厅，男主人脸色阑珊
反穿了拖鞋，白墙上
有女主人疾行中的脚印

carrying a huge barrel of suburban lake on his shoulder
the courier service guy with the leaping eyebrows
his lips show a smear of oily distant hills
the locksmith with a crushed pinky finger
has to work with his thumbs,
pushes aside the springs beneath the leaves
the napping nanny from anhui
keeps fretting about the old widower ·
and the pekinese dog who went with him to heaven

climb with us, stranger
this building's not much more than ten stories high
the pleasure's not much more than ten tons heavy
why the racket, the thicket
all the debts of an unfinished heart
(we've been around the block)
but who hasn't managed to repay it in monthly installments?

but there, *über allen Gipfeln*,
the north wind once advanced its clever lies
we ring the doorbell: explain why we've come
and discover to our surprise: the master bedroom
encases the parlor, the leading man's complexion crumbles,
his slippers are on upside-down, on the white wall
are the leading lady's racing footprints

Also Available from Zephyr Press

Flash Cards
Yu Jian
Translated by Wang Ping & Ron Padgett

The Changing Room
Zhai Yongming
Translated by Andrea Lingenfelter

Doubled Shadows
Ouyang Jianghe
Translated by Austin Woerner

A Phone Call from Dalian
Han Dong
Edited by Nicky Harman
Translated by Nicky Harman, Maghiel van Crevel,
Yu Yan Chen, Naikan Tao, Tony Prince & Michael Day

Wind Says
Bai Hua
Translated by Fiona Sze-Lorrain

I Can Almost See the Clouds of Dust
Yu Xiang
Translated by Fiona Sze-Lorrain

Canyon in the Body
Lan Lan
Translated by Fiona Sze-Lorrain

Something Crosses My Mind
Wang Xiaoni
Translated by Eleanor Goodman

October Dedications
Mang Ke
Translated by Lucas Klein, Huang Yibing
and Jonathan Stalling